Building Mil
Dioramas Vol.VI

CW01669946

VP
the world in scale

Verlinden Publications

COPYRIGHT © 2002 By
Verlinden Productions, Inc.
811 Lone Star Drive
O'Fallon, MO 63366
USA

ISBN : 1-930607-56-3

All rights reserved.

No parts of this book may be reproduced in any form, stored in a retrieval system or transmitted in any form and by any means, be it electronic, mechanical, photocopying or otherwise, without the written consent of the publisher **Verlinden Publications / Verlinden Productions, Inc.**

Published and distributed by
Verlinden Productions, Inc.
811 Lone Star Drive
Lone Star Industrial Park
O'Fallon, MO 63366
USA

Project Manager & Chief Editor : François VERLINDEN
Photography : François VERLINDEN unless otherwise indicated

Editorial Staff : François VERLINDEN
Charlie PRITCHETT
Pat COONEY

Printed in the USA.

CARELESS

By VP Studios

The VP building consists of Ceramic walls, resin roof & shutters, and printed commercial signs. Careful painting & weathering turns it into a convincing French countryside farmhouse.

After gaining a solid foothold along the Normandy coast in France in June 1944, the allies spent all of the following month attempting to break-out of hedgerow country. This was finally achieved by the beginning of August. The following thrusts by the Americans in the south and the British & Canadians in the north ultimately resulted in the encirclement of German forces in the Falaise gap. The encircled Germans tried desperately to break-out of their trap, finally scattering in the countryside to avoid capture and losing most of their equipment to Allied fighter-bombers. Although the major divisions were either destroyed or dismembered, cut-off individual units fought viciously and still posed a deadly threat to the advancing Allies.

Some 'dead space' is filled with vegetation, firewood, wheel barrow, and axe.

This scene shows an American recon group having a break on a French countryside road after the breakout from the Normandy beachhead. One of the GI's is quite interested in the knocked out Tiger I at the roadside while two others take some time to play some ball. The picture is not quite as peaceful as it seems at first glance; A couple of crack SS troops are hiding out behind the farmhouse, ready to strike.

2 sheets of VP Cobblestones are cut to fit the base and painted with a heavy wash of Black, earth, and Green enamels and blended after dry with Scotchbrite.

Top Left
The US tanker is inspecting the hole in the side of the Tiger where the shell impacted the fuel tank & set it ablaze. As it is only partially burnt, the tank must not have been carrying much fuel. Note the charred zimmerit coating, in places pulverized into ashes.

Top
Skybows magnificent Dodge 6x6 is built straight from the box except for the VP cal .50. Note the variety of US gear stowed in and on the vehicle and the tow cable & chain wrapped around the front bumper.

Left
The German squad leader is signalling his comrade to toss a grenade from their concealed position behind the building.

Top view of the Tiger reveals some interesting details such as the distressed air intake screens and tow cables, the gear on the engine deck, the rusty areas where the paint & zimmerit has been burned away and the sooty exhaust stains.

ITEMS USED:

Skybow Dodge 6x6
Tamiya Jeep
Tamiya Tiger I
VP #1145 Cobblestones
VP #1859 European Country House
All figures & accessories VP
Woodland Scenics Foliage

DRY REFUELLING?

By Mig Jimenez

Kit from AFV Club
Tarp & Wheels from Mig Productions

Sometimes I feel the necessity to build a scale model 'out-of-the-box'. A lot of people think that a scale model is correct only if it includes additional photo-etched parts, aluminum gun barrels, individual track sets, and many more extra things not found in the basic kit. But we can not forget that to make models is to have a good time. We can enjoy a simple or a complicated model. Everything is valid. The most important thing is that we should not forget when we were children and enjoyed building our models 'out-of-the-box'. With this SdKfz 11, I have returned to my childhood.

I believe that the AFV Club kit is very good, except some basic details that can easily be corrected, such as the NOTEK support bracket or the rear tow hook. Aside from these minor flaws, I believe this to be a very accurate scale model. In order to make a slightly different version, I used the new tarp & special wheels from Mig Productions. The clean-up of parts is very simple and the instructions include a step-by-step painting guide. I find that this can be of great assistance to many amateur modelers who may have problems in this area.

This SdKfz 11 is set in a place near the Polish frontier in 1944. In an immense field, the driver of the vehicle is trying to get precious fuel to continue his journey along the road, but there is a shortage and he will have to wait for his supplies. This vehicle is decorated with the symbol of the 4th Panzer division using VP dry-transfers (#0232 & #0223).

With very little effort and some very simple painting techniques we can have a finished scale model very quickly. This can motivate us a lot when we are used to spending many months to make a single model.

Special thanks to my Taiwanese friend Max Wang.

PAINTING PHASE

STEP 1 : The AFV Club kit is very accurate, except some small details such as the engine compartment doors. It needs a little extra patience.

STEP 2 : The other black mark on this kit is it's vinyl track. Strangely, we must remove two links from the left track because it is too long. After that, we can glue it with super glue.

STEP 3 : With the resin tarps & wheels, we can dramatically change the look of the SdKfz 11. This is a very fast & easy conversion.

STEP 4 : We apply the base color with an airbrush using a mixture of Tamiya Dark Yellow, White, and clear varnish. For the Green camouflage color a mixture of Vallejo White, Green, and Duck Egg was used.

STEP 5 : The base color of the tarp is a dark Gray, although it can also be a different shade of Green; both are correct. The MP kit includes a step-by-step painting guide for the tarps & wheels.

STEP 6 : We apply a filter with enamel paint using a soft brush. The filter differs from the wash in that it contains a thinner to paint ratio of 95:5, whereas a wash contains much more paint.

STEP 7 & 8 : Next, we make a further alteration of colors by using oils. We apply different points, and later we blend them with a clean brush.

STEP 9 : After the previous application of paint has dried, we use a wash of dark oil colors to pull-out some details such as rivets & hinges.

STEP 10 : First we make chips with a light sand color, using a very fine brush. The chips should be very irregular.

STEP 11 : Here is a general view in the first stage of chipping.

STEP 13 : General look of the chipping phase. In some areas, the chips must be extremely small.

DUST PHASE

STEP 15 : First we should airbrush a very soft layer of dust using a mixture of Tamiya Buff & Flat Earth. This subtle dusting will serve as a base for the application of mud and the more opaque dust.

STEP 12 : Later, we add the rust chips with enamel paints inside of the light color.

STEP 14 : We paint the leather seats with Chocolate enamel color using a paint brush.

STEP 16 : We can fix pigment powder with a paintbrush to simulate realistic dust.

STEP 17: Later, we add clean paint thinner to fix the powder to the surface.

STEP 18 : To make dry mud, we mix stucco, sand, and earth pigments and apply it with an old paintbrush.

STEP 19 : The appearance of the mix is that of real mud!

STEP 20 : Now, we apply the mixture to the hull, wheels, and front parts.

STEP 21 : For the wheels, we again use Mig Productions pigments. First the wheel is painted in a Gray color. After applying the pigments, we clean the excess dust with a soft cloth.

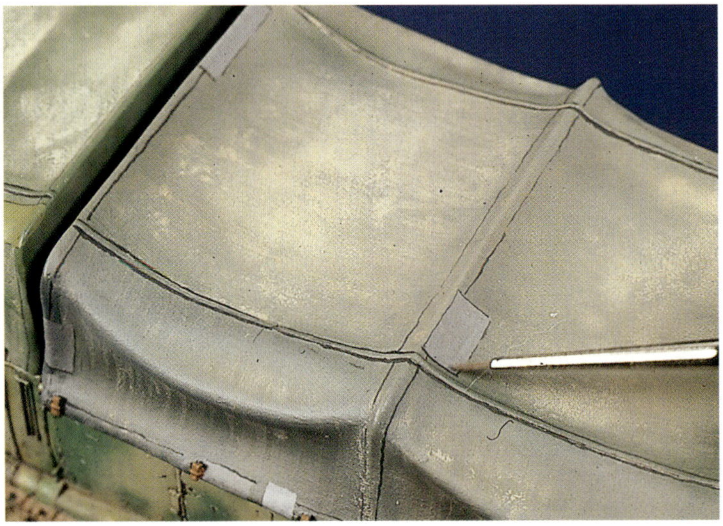

STEP 22 : We paint the tarp following the instructions in the kit.

STEP 23 : We must take care to leave some clean areas, like the big chipped fenders.

STEP 24 : To simulate the dirty water run-downs, we mix satin varnish and Brown enamels and draw them vertically down with a brush.

STEP 25 : General view of the finished model. Even with the heavy dust, we can see the camouflage.

STEP 26 : Irregularity is very important in the painting phases. The dirty stains is one such example.

STEP 27 : Pay attention to the dirt on the wheels. Some parts are clean, and other parts are dirty.

STEP 28 : The base was built with putty and covered with sand and small stones.

STEP 29 : White glue was used to secure the sand & small stones.

STEP 31 : After applying some dark washes, a light colored dry-brush is applied.

STEP 33 : The soldier is opening the door. The mud on his trousers is made from pigments like that on the vehicle.

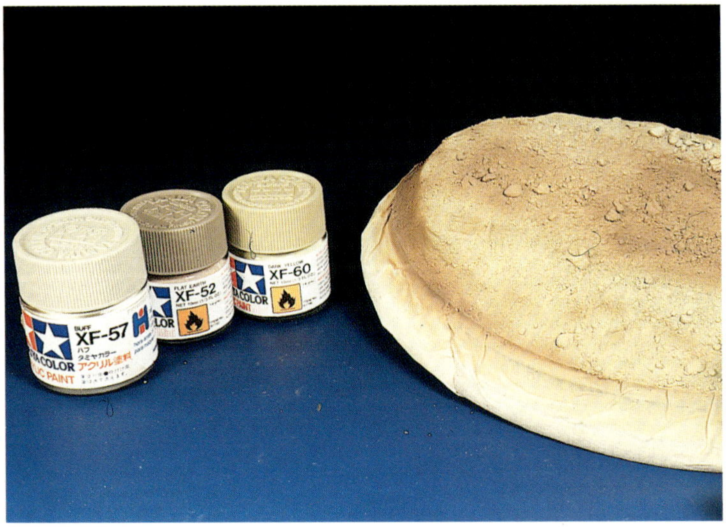

STEP 30 : The base color was airbrushed using Tamiya colors.

STEP 32 : The figure was converted from Warriors and has a Hornet head. It was painted with Vallejo colors.

STEP 34 : It's important to adapt the tracks to the earth in order to represent the weight of the vehicle.

STEP 36 :A little inclination in the base could be an interesting way to show the model. Usually, the modeler displays his kit on a flat base. With a little more work, we can make an original presentation like this one.

HUEY DOWN

By VP Studios

The Vietnam War saw the use of a great variety of American weapon systems, but it will always be remembered as "The Helicopter War". The reason is that prior to Vietnam, helicopters were not deployed in as many roles or in as many numbers in any conflict. In Vietnam, the US Army first went 'airmobile'. Helicopters were used to bring the first 'overt' US ground troops into battle in Vietnam, and they were used to evacuate the last US troops from Vietnam 11 years later. It can easily be concluded that the Vietnam war could not have been fought effectively without the heavy use of helicopters. All sorts of helicopters were used, but none stand out as much as the ubiquitous UH-1 Huey.

Inspired by Don Greer's illustration on the cover of squadron/signal's "Bent & Battered Rotors" Volume 3, VP Studios attempted to recreate this scene of a crashed Huey gunship in a rice paddy.

The heavily weathered Huey riddled with bullet holes from heavy machine gun fire sits in the muddy rice paddy. The crew & passengers are under enemy fire behind the cover of the dikes.

The basic set-up using a piece of polyfoam edged with strips of styrene sheet. The dikes are thin strips of polyfoam shaped with a soldering iron and blended into the base with tile grout cement. A hole in the foam was shaped to fit the helicopter.

A closer view during the onstruction of the dikes. The banks are covered with VP Static Grass tapped into the wet groundwork.

A closer look at the Huey model reveals the heavy weathering of the machine and the impacts of the enemy machine gun. Holes are drilled first, edges jagged with a knife, and chipped paint simulated with aluminum paint.

The muddy bed of the paddy was first built-up with tile grout cement spread out with a wet brush and then painted with various shades of Brown and Khaki tones. Holes were punched in the polyfoam to receive the rice plants, which were cut from a cheap paintbrush. After dry, a coat of Envirotex Lite was poured on to represent the glossy water surface.

The GI's in cover behind the dikes are returning fire while trying to hold their position. Note the lower legs look wet. A thinned transparent coat of very dark Green and a few coats of Future floor wax works great for this effect.

The GI Vietnam (VP 1625) was made for such a diorama as this, plunging his way through the deep mud. The vegetation on the dikes in various tones of Green brings some much needed color variation to an otherwise monotone scene. Also note how deep the chopper went into the mud on one side.

The wounded pilot being treated was built into the groundwork before applying paint and the Envirotex gloss coat for better integration into the scene. Also note the rifle cartridge cases just under the water surface, resting on the muddy bottom.

Items used:

MRC UH-1C Huey Gunship
VP 0399 US Squad Leader Vietnam
VP 0444 Law Gunner Vietnam (discontinued)
VP 0452 M79 Grenade Gunner Vietnam (discontinued)
VP 0480 US Riflemen Vietnam
VP 1430 US Marines Vietnam
VP 1625 GI Vietnam

REFERENCES:
Bent & Battered Rotor's, Vol.3
squadron/signal publications

Airmobile: The Helicopter War in Vietnam
squadron/signal publications

THE RECOVERY

By VP Studios

Much experience is required to build a scene like this. One must master many skills, including building, painting & weathering armor models, painting figures & animals, constructing groundwork with vegetation, mud, and water. This feature will reveal some advice and basic techniques.

The basic base was cut from a piece of blue polyfoam and a thinner piece of the same was glued on top for forming the river bank. The sides were sanded smooth with a sanding block and strips of plastic were glued to the sides high enough to create a reservoir to contain the water. Next, an area was cut out of the styrofoam to fit the model. All gaps were filled in with mud, and mud was added over the ground.

Most dioramas start with an idea or a story. This one started with a product. The VP Elephant with Children is a great new item, opening a whole range of possibilities for something different on many Vietnam dioramas & vignettes. We wanted to create a scene to show the contrast between modern artificial power and the natural power used for many centuries by Asian cultures. This M113 got stuck in a muddy riverbed and no other vehicles are immediately available in the area. Two Vietnamese children passing by with their elephant turned out to be a perfect recovery vehicle.

The vehicle commander and a GI are watching the recovery operation from the side. Also note the old, rusted VP chain. The rust was achieved by soaking the chains in a chemical rusting agent.

The beautifully sculpted elephant is a joy to build & paint. Gray oils were used in various tones with Raw Umber oils for dark shadows. Note that these animals were chained at the front legs, with some slack, to prevent them from running too fast.

The M113 version used here is a conversion of the basic Tamiya kit fitted with side and rear firing ports. Although it was an experimental version, some were tested in Vietnam.

A good overview shows the effective jungle vegetation. The groundwork started by roughing up the polyfoam with a soldering iron and covered with a layer of grout cement textured with an old paintbrush. Static grass was sprinkled over the wet cement on both sides of the muddy trail. Footprints were made by pushing the elephant into the wet groundwork. The whole thing was allowed to dry overnight before base coating all surfaces (including the riverbed) with Dark Earth acrylic paint. After drying, the static grass was dry-brushed with different shades of Greens and the trail & riverbank were dry-brushed with different shades of Earth. VP palm trees, palm plants, painted aquarium plants, roots, Woodland Scenics fine leaf foliage and various florists dried plants were built-up into a realistic composition.

The final operation was to achieve a wet, muddy effect on the river bank and trail. A few coats of Future floor wax did wonders!

Top view of the M113 reveals it's various stowage of ammo cases, weapons, and equipment. Also clearly visible are the fuel & oil stains in the water, which were accomplished by dropping a few drops of Humbrol matt Black into the uncured resin water.

To simulate the vehicle 'waterline', 2 coats of Future floor wax were painted on, darkening the paint and simultaneously adding a semigloss finish. Also note the branches (roots) in the water, which is slightly transparent at the top layer.

Items used:
Envirotex Lite resin
Tamiya M113
VP 0044 Static Grass
VP 0058 Palm plants
VP 0078 Palm Trees
VP 0255 Flower Power
VP 0620 Heavy Tow Chain
VP 1543 Elephant with Children
VP 1585 Vehicle Stowage Set US Vietnam
Woodland Scenics Fine leaf Foliage

Envirotex Lite was mixed and colored with a mix of Humbrol Matt Earth (29), Green (105), and Yellow resulting in a dirty light olive. This was slowly poured into the reservoir for the river until it was about 2mm deep. After drying, a clear coat of about 0.5mm finished the water surface creating a slightly transparent effect at the surface.

BROKEN

By Greg Cihlar

It has been a couple of years since I have made a 1/15 scale diorama, so after looking through book after book for that one picture that will kick my imagination into gear, I found "German Armored Units at Arnhem" by Concord publications. This book is packed with an impressive amount of pictures that inspire diorama ideas and, since I've wanted to build the big VP Stug for awhile, it was a perfect match. While there isn't a picture of a Stug IIIF/8 in this book, who's to say there weren't any of them in that theater in that area? Since I seem to be on a knocked-out vehicle kick lately, I chose a scene where a Stug had made a wrong turn while being chased by U.S. Airborne forces and had crashed through a fence and over a ledge, breaking it's track and drive sprocket. With the release of the two 101st Airborne figures from VP, I imagined using them in a scene where they had just captured the tank and were extracting the crew.

This view provides an excellent perspective of the careful composition of this large scale diorama.

Seeing the unpainted diorama allows us to see how it was built-up with various materials & mediums.

The model was camouflaged with Tamiya acrylics using an airbrush.

The torsion bars, road wheels, and tracks were assembled to conform with the base, depicting a thrown track.

The model was carefully modified to fit the custom base. Note that the broken drive sprocket is embedded into the groundwork for maximum realism.

Here is the completely painted & weathered model ready to be placed on the base.

The basic groundwork before painting. Note the track impressions on the road, representing a well travelled road.

This side provides an excellent view of the damaged flower bed.

I started out with a piece of 5/8" plywood cut to fit the scene; this is always important, to make your base fit the diorama, not to have the diorama fit a base which is too big or too small for the scene you are trying to create. In this case, the plywood was cut to 18" x 16", then built-up with pieces of different thicknesses of styrofoam. After this was secured with glue & screw, I applied 2 thin coats of plaster to the concrete wall section. After it dried, this area was sanded down and the expansion joints were scribed in. Next I applied a base of Celluclay to the road and garden areas. For the road, I covered the entire area with patches of small rock and sand. While this was still wet, I pressed the tracks into it to give the impression of a well-travelled road.

Breaking through the gate literally stopped this tank in it's tracks!

The finished fence. Note the damage to the concrete sections caused by the speeding tank.

then assembled and glued in place. The fenders were then glued in place and the entire tank was sprayed using Black auto body spray paint. The tank was then set aside to dry for approximately 1 hour. I wanted to make a Yellow/Brown camouflage scheme, so I started by applying a base coat of Tamiya Khaki in a cloud pattern, concentrating on the centers of every panel and section, then fading out towards the edges of the panels. I then used Tamiya Dark Yellow following the same pattern until I had a balance between highlights and the depth of shadows in the corners and around some of the more detailed parts. Next I made a mix of Tamiya Red Brown and Hull Red and airbrushed a thin but busy camouflage pattern. I then set the model aside for a few hours to dry. After dry, I started to weather and apply a chipped paint effect. This was done by using a small rounded dull craft knife starting on the edges of each section and gently scraping the paint off in a quick but random motion. By using this technique, the black spray paint primer was exposed. This process was done more heavily on the top of the hull and around hatches and other high traffic

For the garden, I used miscellaneous dried flowers to make the foliage. This was also pressed into place while the groundwork was still wet. For the two columns that support the fence, I started with styrofoam cut to size and then plastered and scribed as before. The ornament on top is from a local craft store. The fence sections were made from scratch using styrene stock.

The entire base was then covered with diluted white glue and set aside to dry for two days. Next, the road and garden sections were sprayed a Black/Brown mix and the dried flowers were sprayed with Tamiya Flat Red. The concrete sections and columns were sprayed a Gray-Brown mix, then washed with Raw Umber and dry-brushed with Payne Gray and White oils. The fence sections were sprayed with Flat Black then lightly dusted with Tamiya Dark Yellow, then washed with Raw Umber and dry-brushed with Model Masters Armor sand. The road section was dry-brushed using different shades of Khaki and Tan until the right dusty, dried dirt appearance was achieved.

The Stug was built without any major problems until I came to the conclusion that I needed to open the hatches. I started by making copies of the hatches using plastic card. Next came the drilling, cutting, and sanding of the two hatch openings in the upper hull. After the basic shape was achieved, I glued plastic card to form a smooth interior wall. Next, the road wheels were positioned and glued in place to represent the angle in which the tank would be positioned. The track was

The paratroopers waste no time in apprehending the tank crew.

The paint chipping was executed by scraping away the top layers of camouflage colors to reveal the Flat Black primer underneath.

areas, as this is where more wear & tear would be on the real thing. The fenders also received a similar treatment on their edges. After I got the look I wanted, I gave the entire tank a wash of Raw Umber and Burnt Sienna oils thinned with paint thinner, taking care not to brush over any of the chipped areas (which would reactivate the Black primer). This was then set aside to dry overnight. Next I dry-brushed the tank with Model Masters Armor sand. I finished it off with a very light dry-brushing of a mix of Silver printer's ink & Raw Umber oils. This is a case where less is more. I applied the mud in the usual way, mixing Celluclay, white glue, and sand, followed by washing & dry-brushing. The tracks were rusted using Modern Options rust finish, then toned-down with three washes of Raw Umber thinned again with paint thinner.

The VP paratroopers are a perfect fit for this diorama, albeit with a few minor modifications.

Note the extensive dirt caked onto the rear of the tank.

FIGURES

The American standing on the ground is VP #1764, and was built straight from the box without any modifications. The American holding the Thompson MG is VP #1788, which was slightly converted to hold the gun at a lower angle, and was given a new head from the spares box. The American holding the pistol is a conversion of VP #1764, with an adjusted right arm and new hand from VP #0549 assorted hand set, and the left leg cut at the knee and repositioned & blended-in with Milliput to achieve a more aggressive pose. The German laying on the ground was made using the upper body & arms from an old Kirin figure, with a new head from Warriors and legs made from Milliput & VP boots from the spares box. The German on the tank is a mix of VP parts from VP #0959 German Tank Crew, and a head from the discontinued VP#1078 Volksturm figure. The Germans were painted using a mix of Dark Grey and Khaki, then dry brushed with Medium and Light Greens. All three Americas were painted using a base of Light Brown, then oversprayed with tamiya Khaki & dry brushed with assorted Khaki & Tan oils. The skin tones for all of the figures were painted in oils.

Photographed in front of a suitable backdrop, this diorama is dramatic indeed!

Into the Reich

By VP Studios

January 1945, near the German border. It's cold, wet, Icy, and foggy; not exactly a day for a sightseeing trip. US troops are moving into Germany, engaging in the final battles of WWII in Europe.

Note here how the tank is moving to the right to pass the roadblock. The wet and icy look is done with several coats of spray adhesive (before adding the model, figures, and accessories). Some Woodland Scenics snowflakes were sprinkled on to achieve a more convincing winter effect.

The basic set-up of the scene. The VP Castle Remains is built, painted, and weathered separately before building it into the groundwork, as are the cobblestone sections. A piece of polyfoam is glued onto the base and shaped with a soldering iron, The groundwork is built-up with tile grout mortar. Rubble and larger parts fallen from the ruin are pressed into the wet groundwork, followed by the addition of static grass.

Below
A picture with a suitable background creates an even more convincing atmosphere of a cold winter morning.

Various arms & equipment (all VP accessories) are littered in and around the ruins. Note the small arms cartridge cases, cut from brass wire.

The Sherman tank loaded with infantry is moving past a road block. Some fighting must have occurred just before. Testimony are the dead German soldier and the remains of weapons and the many spent cartridge cases in and around the foxhole.

Military modelers have been so many times accused of glamorizing war. What we are doing is studying and rebuilding history in scale in the most realistic way. War is horror, death, and destruction, and that is also part of the same history. Ignoring this fact would in fact be glamorizing war. Some might call this picture "bad taste", but it is simply depicting the reality of war.

A view from the back reveals the debris and the abandoned German resistance nest. Roots are used for trees and branches, some being used to camouflage the foxhole.

Small items fill the dead space at the front. A wooden beam used for the roadblock. A roadblock fence with barbed wire and some cartridge cases. Also note the patches of ivy on the ruins made by sprinkling tea leaves into the white glue,painted dark Green after dry and drybrushed with various lighter Green shades.

A closer look at the GI's crouched together on the engine deck. Not a very comfortable ride, but at least it's warm. Note the various gear.

A good photo of the heavily weathered Sherman tank showing a fading winter whitewash. A complete guide to weathering this model can be seen in the VP Publication 'Military Vehicles Vol.III'.

Items used:

Tamiya Sherman

VP 1145 Cobblestones
VP 1180 US Infantry ETO
VP 1586 US Tank Crew Wet/Cold
VP 1683 US Tank Riders Set 1
VP 1686 US Tank Riders Set 2
VP 1777 German Casualties
VP 1865 Castle Remains
All other accessories VP

SUEZ STINGER

Egyptian SA-6 'Gainful' October 1973

By Charlie Pritchett

The improvised infantry 'Sagger' emplacement was easily made with a few VP 55 gallon drums, some VP corrugated plastic sheet, and Milliput sandbags.

The Soviet SA-6 is an area defense tactical surface-to-air missile system based on the ZSU-23-4 'Shilka' AA chassis, which is in turn derived from the chassis of the ASU-85. In battle, the SA-6 works in conjunction with the 'Long Track' and 'Straight Flush' Radar systems. To engage a target, the 'Long Track' radar first detects the target and transmits information such as bearing, range, and altitude, to the 'Straight Flush' radar system, which in turn carries out limited search, low altitude detection/acquisition, target tracking and illumination, missile radar command guidance and secondary radar missile tracking functions. The 'Straight Flush' locates the target and, if this is confirmed as hostile, locks on to it using it's tracking and illumination radars. Once this has been achieved the radar changes to the continuous-wave mode and a missile is launched. The missile receives & transmits data back to the 'Straight flush' radar until it reaches the terminal homing stage, which is of the semi-active radar type. At this point the first stage of the missile is ejected and the ramjet engine kicks in. The warhead is fitted with a proximity fuse and an impact fuse, so it does not necessarily require a direct hit in order to destroy the target. The 550kg (1,212 Ib) solid-propellant rocket-ramjet 9M9 missile carries a 80 kg (176 Ib) HE fragmentation warhead at speeds reaching mach 2.8 to a low-altitude range of 60 km (37 miles) and a high-altitude range of 30 km (18 miles).

The model was painted with mixtures of Model Masters enamels. The tactical markings were hand-painted, as well as the rubber tires on the road wheels.

This view shows the hull after the filters were applied. Notice the slight change of color from the stock finish.

Here we can see the addition of the 'chipped paint' effect. This was tediously applied by hand with the corresponding underlying colors. Note that since the dark Olive camouflage color is applied over 2 colors, first Sand and then Russian Green, the chips on this color can reflect this.

Manufactured in the U.S.S.R in the 1960's, the SA-6 first drew blood in service with the Egyptian & Syrian armies during the Yom Kippur/Ramadan war of 1973. The Egyptians undertook a massive disinformation campaign under the guise of training exercises so as to catch the Israelis off-guard...and it worked! The Egyptian plan called for a bridgehead across the Suez canal to be established for each of it's 5 invading infantry divisions within the first few hours. These would allow all of the infantry battalions and all of their support to deploy into Sinai to cover the armor & artillery crossings. Anti-tank teams armed with 'Sagger' ATGW's and RPG-7's prepared ambushes and laid mines in preparation for the expected Israeli counter-attack. To protect their ground forces from Israeli ground-support attacks, the Egyptians protected their invading armor with a dense anti-air network. The Egyptians set-up their SAM's in a classic Soviet concept of layered air defenses, so that the tactics to evade one system would bring the attacking Israeli aircraft into the envelope of others.

In addition to deploying the SA-6, the Egyptians also made effective use of the tried SA-2 'Guideline' SAM, the man-portable shoulder-launched SA-7 'Grail'

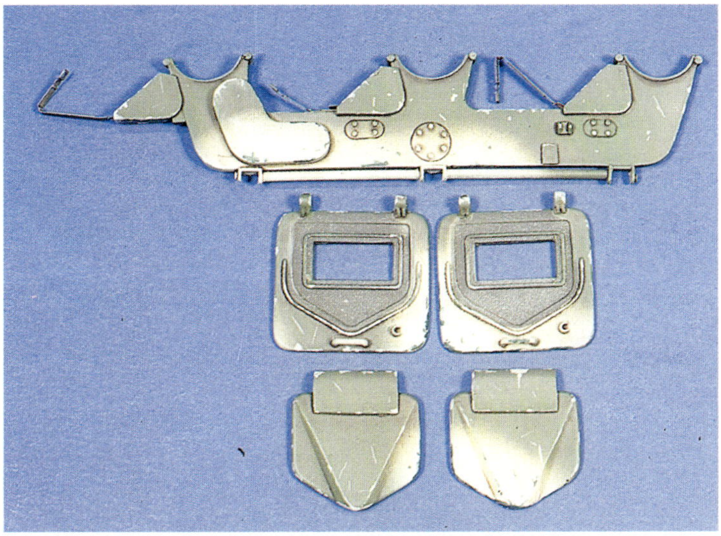

The travel lock & hatches were painted separately in the same manner as the hull & launcher.

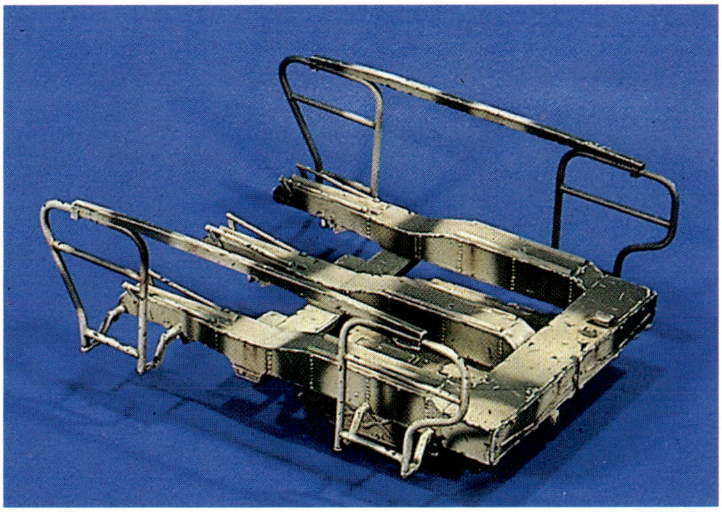

This is a view of the missile launcher turret after applying the filters, 'chipped paint' and rust stains.

At this stage of 'weathering', the model has already taken on a much more dynamic appearance, but more is still needed...

After adding the 'chipped paint' effect, rust stains were added with artists oils.

units, as well as the ZSU-23-4 'Shilka' AA gun systems. In all, the SA-6 claimed some 40 victims in service with the Egyptians during the intense conflict. However, by the end of the conflict, and due to Egyptian over-extension, the Israelis managed to over-run some Egyptian SAM sights and capture several examples of the SA-6, resulting in the development of effective countermeasures against the lethal system.

The model depicted here represents that first deployed by Egypt during the 1973 war (later Egyptian examples show a new camouflage color & pattern). The color scheme consists of a sand color applied over the original Soviet dark Green, with a camouflage pattern of another dark Green over the Sand color. It is presumed that the undersurfaces of the hull were not painted by the Egyptians, retaining the original Soviet dark Green. The 9M9 missiles are all painted in dark Green, but all in slightly different shades to simulate different production batches or suppliers (that's my story and I'm sticking to it!). I researched this model thoroughly, and the experts tell me that the war-rounds are painted in dark Green, with White warheads. Inert practice rounds are White with Blue or Gray warheads. I have also seen Iraqi examples that are overall white...I opted for the green/white as advised by the experts...just to be safe!

The basic model is the Dragon ZSU-23-4M with the Cromwell Models SA-6 conversion. In the end, the only Dragon parts used were the lower hull and some minor fittings such as the pioneer tools & tow shackles. Because the SA-6 hull is longer than that of the ZSU-23/4, Cromwell provides a plug which must be sandwiched between the front & rear sections of the Dragon hull (after it is cut in half). This being done, the Cromwell upper-hull fits very neatly onto the modified dragon lower-hull. In order to make my model more convincing, I cut-out the casted-on exhaust grill on the rear plate & made a new one from some spare photo-etched parts. I also made the mud-flaps from lead foil, securing them with styrene strips & bolts behind the drive sprockets, and a few nuts & bolts in various other locations from the punch & die. The Cromwell upper hull is cast with many small fittings & handles, many of which were broken on my example. All of the grab-handles were cut off & replaced by new ones made from copper wire. The very tiny tie-down rings along the upper edges of the hull sides were replaced by new rings I found in a model train hobby shop. The rings appear to be used to secure a protective tarpaulin in place. The pioneer tools were secured with small bits of photo-etch. The most challenging aspect of this model is the missile rack. Unfortunately, Cromwell doesn't provide any instruction or reference to make these, so I resorted to scratch-building my own using various photographs as a reference. The four elements of the racks were made from a stiff wire coated with plastic available from Plastruct, and the

MIG Productions powdered pigments were used to simulate the accumulated dust in the corners & recesses.

Applying a coat of 'dust' to the model helped to tone it down & place it in the desert. Thinned Tamiya acrylics were airbrushed along the hull sides & running gear before selectively applying MP pigments.

connecting bars were made from Evergreen styrene strip & rod. Attaching these delicate racks to the model was frustrating because they continuously broke-off. The missiles themselves had incorrectly shaped warheads, which were easily sanded to the correct shape & point. For a more accurate model, I did resort to using some after-market items. The most important addition here was the beautiful set of tracks, road wheels, & sprockets from Modelkasten. The steel tow cables are from Hudson & Allen Studios, and the antenna base is from the old VP T-55 Update Set.

The model was painted with mixtures of Model Masters enamels. I mixed my own colors because I could not find the exact colors I was looking for in the jars. I started by coating the entire model with a Raw Umber primer. This darkened it very much, and provided a form of 'pre-shading'. In the end this may not have been necessary. The next color was an overall Russian dark Green, which would have been the original color of the vehicle. I followed with an overall light Sand color. Although it is invisible, I did leave the bottom of the hull and the backs of the road wheels in the Russian Green. I doubt the Egyptians would bother to paint these areas. The next color to be applied was a dark Olive Green in a camouflage pattern. I studied many photos of Egyptian SA-6 and other vehicles to get a feel for the camouflage styles applied. The final painting phase was to color the rubber tires Flat Black, and to paint the markings of the Egyptian Army by hand.

I began 'weathering' the model by adding 2 filters. The first was Burnt Sienna oils, the second was Blue enamels. These very slightly changed the tone of the underlying colors. Next came a very thin overall wash mixed from Burnt Sienna & Raw Umber oils. After this dried, I dry-brushed the entire model with lighter shades of the underlying camouflage colors, again mixed from oils. This was very subtle, only to allow the highlights to stand out. The recess around the turret on the upper hull was given several coats of rust colors mixed from oils. I did this to add some color to the vehicle, and it would be a natural water trap on the real thing. However, I felt that I overdid it a bit, so later in the weathering phase I repaired it with concentrations of dust. The next step was to add the scratches & chips to the

Raising the missile launcher not only adds drama to the model, but also creates some vertical balance to the display.

Viewing this photo, one can only imagine the amount of dust kicked-up when the missiles launch skyward.

paint finish. I used the same colors as when I painted it, but was very careful in their placement. The Sand color was chipped with the Russian Green color. The Olive Green camouflage color was chipped first with the Sand color, then with the Russian Green. Some of the Sand colored chips have Russian Green chips underneath them. All of the chips & scratches were applied to heavy use areas using a very fine brush. The final chip color was a dark Rust color, which was applied just on the corners & edges of parts. This process was very tedious and time consuming, but necessary for realism. Now the model was very dynamic with color, but still not quite realistic to me. The final weathering step was to make it dirty. The Egyptians used their SA-6 in a desert environment, and they used it heavily during the war. When the missile fired, it kicked-up an enormous amount of dust. When the vehicle drove at speed, it also kicked-up lots of dust. So I added lots of dust! This was done by first airbrushing a very thin layer mixed from Tamiya Buff & Desert Yellow overall, concentrating more on the lower areas around the wheels & tracks, and also the rear plate. At first this frightened me because it removed the harsh richness of the colors I worked so hard to apply before. Later, after looking at it for an hour or so, I got adjusted to the appearance. Finally I added more concentrated dust to the corners & recesses along the upper surfaces. This was done by mixing MIG Productions pigment colors until I found the shade I was looking for, then mixing it

Dried foliage was added to simulate the arid desert environment of the Suez region, as well as to fill empty space on the base. The VP 55 gallon drums were 'weathered' with the Rustall system.

with some water. I brushed this 'wash' into the areas that I needed concentrated dust. In less than an hour all dust was dry. Naturally some dust was deposited in undesirable places, but it was easily blended out with a clean, dry brush. Finally, a few heavy use areas were lightly rubbed with graphite to bring a polished steel effect. As the SA-6 was a new vehicle in Egyptian service, I tried not to overdo this.

The tracks were first airbrushed with a thin coat of Raw Umber enamel from Model Masters as a base color. I then applied a very light wash of Burnt Sienna oils. After this was completely dry, I used Black MP pigments to stain the road wheel contact area between the guide teeth. The tread-side of the tracks was given the same wash of dust colored pigments as the model, with dramatic results. The last step on the tracks was to rub graphite powder over the high spots to simulate polished steel.

The missiles were painted a little differently from the vehicle. As the resin was white, I simply masked the warheads with tape before applying the colors. One was given a primer of Rust color. This was treated with liquid masking medium before painting the dark Green color. The other two missiles were painted with a very dark Olive Green. To separate them from each other, I applied different colored filters to each of them. Next all three missiles were washed with oils, then highlighted again with oils. This was not exactly dry-brushing because I was actually applying lighter colors to the missiles and blending them together. Because I could not apply liquid masking medium to all of the edges of the missile realistically, I used a brush to add all of the smaller chips & scratches to the missile with a Red primer undercoat. The decal stripes were added last in accordance with photo references. The final effect was to differentiate the missiles from each other and add some interest.

"Cocky" from their resounding victory in the 1967 war, Israeli pilots suffered heavy casualties from this new & unexpectedly formidable weapon system in 1973.

UNDER FIRE
By VP Studios

This dramatic battle scene is situated early in 1945 during the fierce final battles precluding the collapse of the Third Reich, depicting German infantry covered by a Tiger II advancing through a bombed-out town under heavy fire from the rear. This diorama shows all the drama and horror of war; cold. Wet. Desperation, death and destruction.

The base from a piece of polyfoam is fitted with sections of VP Cobblestones forming the street base. The cobblestones are pre-weathered by first applying a wash mix of Humbrol Matt 29 Earth + Black over the bare resin, and later, after dry the whole surface is thoroughly worked over with Scotchbrite.

Below : The pre-painted & weathered building glued to the base with the surrounding debris roughly built-up and shaped.

The groundwork completed and base-coated with a Black/Brown mix of acrylic paint. VP Red Bricks Building sections fill the groundwork, as well as plenty of cat-litter and fine grit.

Left : The scene is ready to receive the snow, tank, figures, and accessories. The base-coated debris is first dry-brushed a Dark Earth color, working gradually lighter with various Grays and Off-Whites. Red Brick is painted in thinned Red-Brown and an overall final dry-brush run of a dust color. Note the oil spills in the middle of the street.

A background photograph of billowing black smoke adds drama and realism to the inferno.

A crewmember brings his comrade into the protective cover of the building. Note the propaganda posters and various road signs.

The tank crew members are taking cover behind the turret while trying to figure out where the shots are coming from so that they can return fire.

For this soldier lying in a pool of blood, any help comes too late.

To simulate snow, baking soda was sprinkled on the base and dispersed with a soft brush. All pre-painted items are glued in place after test fitting until the right balance is achieved.

The inside of the building shows the remains of the roof and floors. A few pieces of furniture, a painting, and a sink were included to add interest.

The officer shot in the leg crawls to safety behind the tank as a rifleman covers him and other soldiers rush in for assistance.

ITEMS USED:

Tamiya
#35169 German King Tiger 'Porsche Turret'

VP
#1145 Cobblestone Street
#1447 Red Bricks
#1533 Ruined Building Sections
All figures, roadsigns, posters, accessories, and country house VP.

See Verlinden Publications #1816 Building, Painting & Weathering Military Vehicles Vol. III for step-by-step painting & weathering of the King Tiger model.

Military Dioramas

We followed up our two popular Aircraft and Military Vehicles series with another promising new series: Building Military Dioramas. Our Volume I brings another 48 pages illustrated with over 100 new full color photographs covering the following subjects:

- Building diorama bases and groundwork
- "Cornered" A WWII combat diorama by VP Studios
- Battle of the Bulge 1944, by VP Studios
- The Railroad Crossing. An instant diorama by VP Studios
- The Farmyard. By VP Studios
- Hamburger Hill Vietnam, May 1969. By Young Jin Won
- "Foto fur die Heimat" By VP Studios
- "Retreat from Budapest" By Greg Cihlar

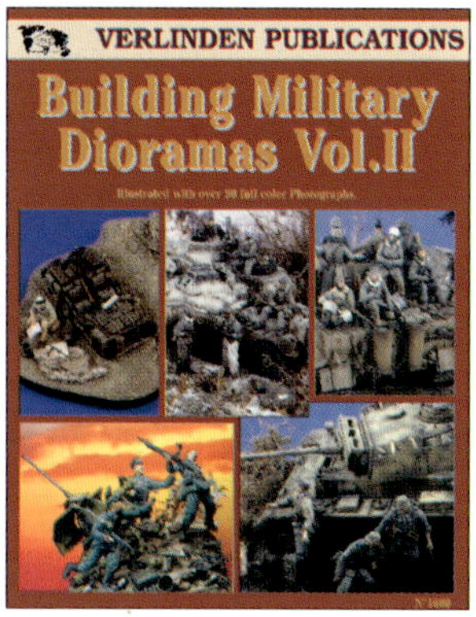

Volume II of our Building Military Dioramas series brings another 48 pages illustrated with over 90 full color photographs covering the following subjects:

- "The Forgotten War", a Korean War diorama by VP Studios
- "Road to Moscow" Operation Barbarossa, by VP Studios
- "Tiger in the Woods", by VP Studios
- "Trouble in France", a 120mm diorama by Greg Cihlar
- "Lost and Found", a 1:35 scale diorama by Greg Cihlar
- "Battlefield", a 1:35 scale vignette by Young Jin Won
- "Desert Raiders" a british SAS vignette by VP Studios
- "Bridge Too Small" by VP Studios

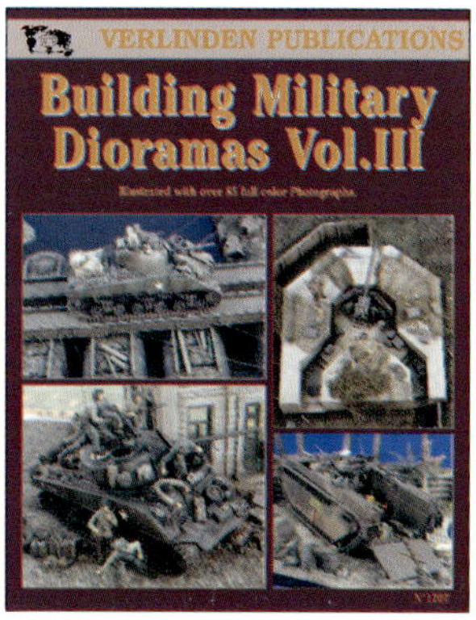

Our Volume III of our Building Military Dioramas series brings another 48 pages loaded with more than 85 full color photographs covering the following breathtaking dioramas from VP Studios:

-The Beach, featuring the LVT-4 with full interior from VP
-Achtung Tieffliegerl, A ready-made diorama base from VP
-Atlantik Wall I: Concrete Gun Emplacement
-The Crossing, featuring the new U.S. Pontoon bridge from VP
-Shadows of the Past: Germany, early 1945
-No Way Out, a Sherman tank diorama by Young Jin Won
-Atlantik Wall II: Gun & Observation Post
-Streetfighters: Battle for a German town, 1945

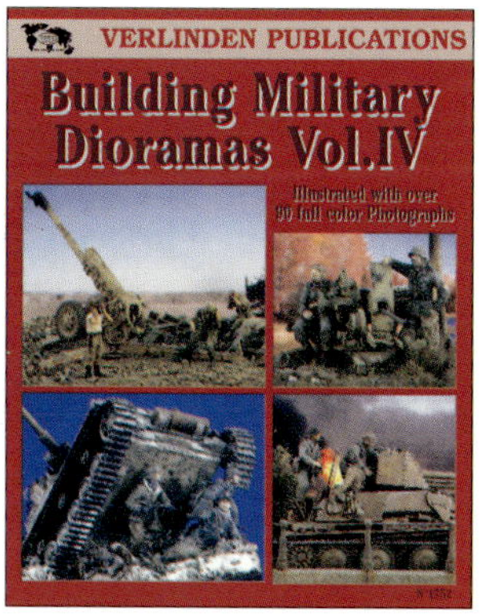

Volume IV of our Building Military Dioramas series brings another 48 pages illustrated with over 90 full color photographs covering the following subjects:

- "DEFENDING THE FAITH", an Iran-Iraq war diorama by Charlie Pritchett
- "SMOKED OUT" June 6, 1944, D-Day, by VP Studios
- "CHECK POINT", a small German vignette by Greg Cihlar
- "CROSSING INTO RUSSIA" over a wooden bridge, by VP Studios
- Painting a Camel, by VP Studios
- "Desert Encounter" with bedouins, by VP Studios
- "UNDER THE TRACKS", a diorama with a German Elefant, by Greg Cihlar
- "MARDER IN ACTION", a step-by-step diorama by VP Studios
- "CROUCHING SOLDIERS", a winter WWII German diorama by Greg Cihlar

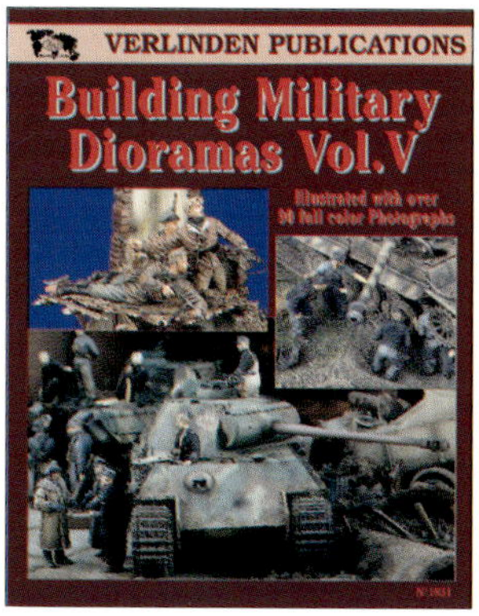

Volume V of our popular Building Military Dioramas series returns with another 48 pages illustrated with over 90 beautiful full color photographs covering the following subjects:

- "COFFEE WITH MILK, PLEASE" Normandy countryside, Summer 1944, with a PzIV zimmerit by VP Studios
- "EVACUATION", A large German diorama with 2 Panthers by Greg Cihlar
- "PAYBACK TIME" Afghanistan 2001, with a BMP-1 by VP Studios
- "MINENSCHADEN", A Tiger track-repair diorama by Robert Döpp
- "BREAKFAST AT THE FRONT", an atmospheric scene with the Marder III by Greg Cihlar
- "RUNNING SCARED" Berlin, April 1945, a vignette by Young jin Won
- "DIRECTIONS", featuring the M10 tank Destroyer lost in the forest, by Greg Cihlar
- "DEADLOCK?" A German siege on a Russian city, by VP Studios
- "FROM THE INSIDE" Berlin, April 1945, another amazing vignette by Young Jin Won

A special edition in our Military Dioramas series, Greg Cihlars Fabulous Military Dioramas features the incredible work by this renowned modeler. This special edition has 36 pages illustrated with over 100 full color photographs, featuring the following subjects:

- "Captured Goods", with a highly detailed M8 "Greyhound" armored car
- "Under the Bridge", a concealed "King Tiger"
- "Warsaw Uprising", with the massive "Stürmtiger"
- "Wacht an Rein", a 120mm "King Tiger"
- "Street Fighters", a small based vignette
- "Defending the Ruhr", featuring the "Jagdpanther"
- "Death from Below" (Berlin 1945), an amazing multi-level sewer diorama
- "Holand 1944", with a German anti-aircraft half-track conversion

Ask for these at your local Hobbyshop or visit Amazon.com Keyword Verlinden